Legal & Disclaimer

The information contained in this book is not designed to replace or take the place of any form of medication or professional medical advice. The information in this book has been provided for educational and entertainment purposes only.

The information contained in this book has been compiled from sources deemed reliable, and it is accurate to the best of the Author's knowledge. However, the Author cannot guarantee its accuracy and validity so cannot be held liable for any errors or omissions. Changes are periodically made to this book. You must consult your doctor or get professional medical advice before using any of the suggested remedies, techniques, or information in this book.

Upon using the information contained in this book, you agree to hold harmless the Author from and against any damages, costs and expenses, including any legal fees, potentially resulting from the application of any of the information provided by this guide. This disclaimer applies to any damages or injury caused by the use and application, whether directly or indirectly, of any advice or information presented, whether for breach of contract, tort, negligence, personal injury, criminal intent, or under any other cause of action.

You agree to accept all the risks of using the information presented inside this book. You need to consult a professional medical practitioner in order to ensure you are both able & healthy enough to participate in this program.

Contents

Introduction

In the world today where people are encouraged to explore more and more career opportunities, many fail to comply. The main reason is the fact that people don't try to identify the passion that they have for a specific field. Personality is the key in determining the type of field you should choose to work. If you are an introvert in media industry, you might fail to achieve the outcomes of being relatable due to lack of social communication.

In order to develop a better understanding of how one should approach life and how one should approach people based on their personalities, the suggestions of carrying out the Enneagram test are made. This simple yet unique test might take 10-15 minutes of your time, but it will give you an insight that will last with you for a lifetime. Before getting started with the test, it is important to know what personality is and why it matters. For a layman, a person acting violently is simply an aggressive person but for someone who understands psychology and human mental crisis, it is a serious lack of anger management. In order to make sure that you understand this difference, this book will be based on raising awareness about importance of knowing one's personality and shaping your life around it to make the most out of it.

Personality and needs to understand it

Personality is the psychological construction of a person. It allows a person to act in normal as well as crisis situations. Personality is psychological as well as mental. Personality on the inside is the way a person sees himself. It is based on his aims, hopes, dreams, his conduct of pothers, his views about himself, his values, his goals and his overall perspective about life and his presence in it. The outside personality is the way a person views the world around him. This allows him to deal with the world, respond to people, and deal with the stress and other external stimuli that might affect him in any manner and his perspective of how he sees people and how he wants people to see him.

It is the personality of a person that allows him to be strategic yet decisive in life. If someone has a confusing personality, his lack of decision making will make it hard for him to excel in life. To some people, personality is their reputation. They see it as their reputation which describes them in front of people. Personality is highly linked to the occupational performance of a person. It's hard for an extrovert to be a writer or a thinker because such a person has too much things on his mind and too many things to do and share. Writers are people with introvert personalities at best since they like to share their ideas through their writings in the form of words. The conflict in personality and profession sometimes create a great unease in life.

It is important to underrated personality because it will play a key role in enhancing the occupational performance of a person and determining his career choices. Not only the career and professional life, the personal life can also bear the brunt if there is a conflict of personality in partners. Having someone beside you who has anger management issues is a turmoil, but it became easy to handle and deal with them if a person is aware of the personality type and how to deal with such a personality. There has been a lot of research done by the psychologists to understand personality and how it affects life of a human. In a global world of today where companies hire people based on their personalities, it is important to know what you are offering to the recruiters, you don't want to be an introvert and doing a sales job because your shyness is not going to convince anyone to buy anything from you. In order to understand personality, the Enneagram test is one such tool which is easy and progressive and predicting quite accurate results.

The test is preliminary and offers guidance, but it must not be taken as a prescription to treat your life with. It is like vitamins which are effective to use and will not cause any harm but will surely bring positivity and a different perspective about life into your conscience. Knowing your personality and taking an Enneagram test will help you to create a better approach towards professional life. Learn more about this test in the sections below and take 10 minutes out of your time to take it. Identify your personality type and start building your life around it with a better perspective.

Chapter 1: What is the purpose of an enneagram test?

The Enneagram test is one of the standards developed by the experts to measure the personality types. It is a model which is developed based on the human psychology. The main aim of this model is to identify the topology and the type of personality a person has based on the nine models which are a part of the model. The nine interconnected personality types are based on the theories and the teachings conducted by Bolivian psycho-spiritual teacher Oscar Ichazo in 1950s as well as the Chilean psychiatrist Claudio Naranjo in the 1970s. Naranjo's theories took a great amount of inspiration from the learnings of George Gurdjieff and the Fourth Way tradition.

The main purpose of having this test is to understand the personality of a person in detail. Since there is a lot of confusion as well as complexity linked with the human psychology, it is hard to predict how a person in going to react in a certain situation. This model is a great way to understand why someone reacts in a certain way in a certain situation. People tend to overlook the fact that anger management is a great influencer of the personality of a person. Similarly, other external factors also play a key role in development of personality. Some people react to pain with persistence, while some people start crying while some people start shouting and getting angry. All of these emotions are a clear depiction of the fact that it is the personality of a person that makes them react in a particular manner to a particular stimuli.

In order to understand the test in a better way, it is important to understand the sign of the test which is also known enneagram and is based on the "enneatypes" which are the types of the test. The points of a geometric figure are a clear way to understand how the types are defined while making a clear connection between each type of the test.

The Enneagram test of Personality has been widely taught in the studies of psychology and business management. There are special seminars, conferences, books, magazines, and videos available in the market about how to conduct the test. The main aims of the test in the studies is to gain an insight about how different professionals function into a workplace. This allows to develop greater outlook on the interpersonal-dynamics. By understanding this in terms of the spirituality, it allows to develop a better insight into the states of wellness in human being, the main core and essence of their personality and the development and the enlightenment that comes with a personality. It is the key to develop a better sense of self-awareness, self-understanding and self-development. The Enneagram personality test is the key to create personalities which can later on develop to become leaders and influencers.

The main application of the Enneagram personality test is in the development of personality, offering people to master skills while providing a creative solution for resolution of conflicts, building confidence and offering a useful as well as integral mastery in skills like leadership, emotional intelligence, stress management, conflict resolution, building teams, and trusting one's own abilities. The test is a great way to find skills and opportunities which can be a progressive approach for the future. It has been a useful tool to employ in counseling, psychotherapy, business development, parenting and education for the aim of development, skill enhancement and learning.

An insight into the enneagram sign theory

This section will provide an insight into understanding the Enneagram test in a better way. By understanding how the geometric sign of the theory works, a better understand of the types of the personality will be developed. The Enneagram is a nine-point geometric figure. The figure is composed of an outer circle which has nine points which relates to each personality type. The numbers are in the clockwise direction and are kept an even distance on the circle. The points 9, 3 and 6 are joined together by a triangle made inside the circle. There consists of an irregular hexagon which is used to connect the rest of the points present on the circle. The circle is a sign of the completeness and the integrity of life which humans have to go through. It signifies unity, strength and integrity in its true form. It is split up to show how various classes of humans spend life in various conditions.

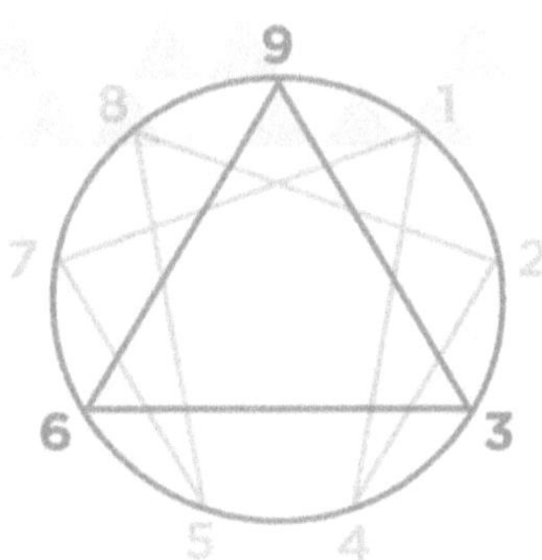

Since there are nine types in total, the type on each side of a single type are named as wings while the central one is known as core. It is known that wings are a representation of interlinked personality types which a person can easily transform himself into. It allows to explore the various facets and factors of life and nature for a person which he can easily transform himself into. It is common for people to have string personality styles of their wings and relatively less of their core. It adds a sense of nuance and integrity to their personality as well as the flexibility to transform according to the situation.

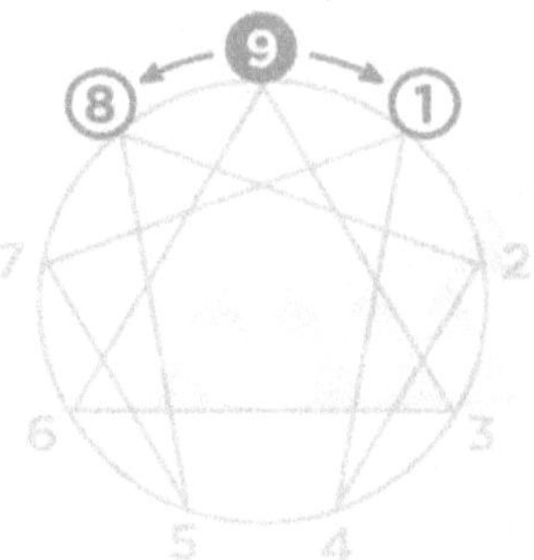

Alongside that, the basic nine personality types are also linked with two lines to two other basic types. For example, the following figure shows the linking of Type 1 to Type 7 and Type 4. It is known that the first line is linked with the type of personality which the human has left or was composed of in the past or earlier in the childhood. The characteristics and features of this type are integral for a person if he eager to develop and grow in his future. The second line is linked with the type of personality which he may compose himself with or grow into in the future. He needs to acquire its features in order to grow into a higher state of personality attainment and growth.

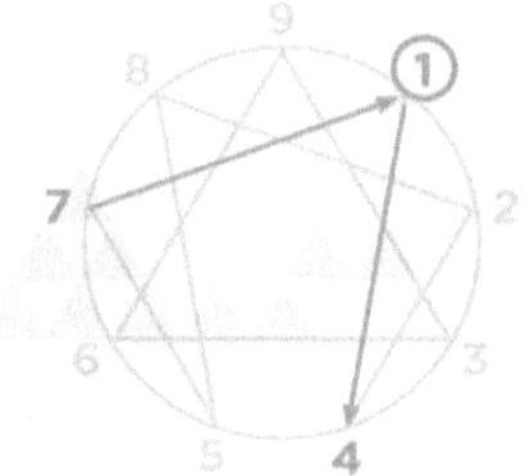

The lines which are shown above depict the basic types of personalities and the weaknesses as well as strengths. But it also highlights the challenges which one has to overcome in order to excel in life. This depicts that personality's not a fac. It might change according to the situation in which a person is put into.

Chapter 2: The simplified 10 minutes enneagram tests you can choose to take

In order to make sure that you get through an Enneagram test which is not only reliable but also provide effective results, you can have multiple options. You will be asked 36 questions with 2 options each. Since there are 36 questions in most tests, the developers tend to change or modify questions. The thing that is highlighted with the Enneagram tests is that you will have tons of tests available on the online from which are free or in some cases charge a little fee. The online tests as well as the pdf Enneagram tests are a great way to test your personality or check the personality of your loved ones.

Enneagram tests to choose from

1.   The Fast Enneagram test

The enneagram test from enneagramtest.net is one of the most valuable and authentic enneagram tests to take. It comes with 36 questions which cover each and every type, ensuring that you are explored from the perspective of each type, allowing to determine the type of personality you have, the wings which your personality possesses and how you might become a better person in the future. The test provide a quick overview of how the other tests of Classical enneagram is carried out. Based on your choices, you will be provided with a result of the personality type that you possess. This is the simplest form of the classical enneagram tests which are available it will hardly take 10 minutes to be completed. https://enneagramtest.net/

2.   The   Riso-Hudson   Enneagram Type

The Riso-Hudson Enneagram Type Indicator comes with 144 questions in the full version which can be easily availed at the rate $10. The sample one is available on their online platforms which can be taken and the personality type will be given. If you have any concern regarding the results from the test, you can consult the Discovering Your Personality Type: The Enneagram Questionnaire by Don Richard Riso and his other related books. In the sample online, there are 38 questions which will hardly tae 10 minutes to complete and you will be provided with the results instantly. https://www.9types.com/rheti/index.php

3. The Integrative Enneagram Questionnaire by Integrative9 Enneagram Solutions

Integrative9's Integrative Enneagram Questionnaire is one of the most valid Enneagram test which provides the perfect Enneagram type as well as the wings, and subtypes. The test will take over 30 minutes which will cost $60+ to get the full results. https://www.integrative9.com/GetYourType/

4. The Enneagram Personality Test by Truity

The Enneagram Personality Test by Truity is one of the tests which will hardly take 10-15 minutes to complete. It is a free test so the results are very vague and it is not very effective but can provide results for personal use. There is no justification for the personality types and no useful is offered by the test but it can be taken for fun purposes. https://www.truity.com/test/enneagram-personality-test

5. Essential Enneagram Online Test by the Narrative Enneagram

The Essential Enneagram assessment by The Narrative Enneagram is one of the best tests based on the personality types available online. The test provides great insight into the personalities, strengths and coping mechanisms which is useful for the people who want to take decisions based on their personalities. The test provides in-depth insight while taking a bit more time as compared to the other online Enneagram tests. You will need to spend 45-60 minutes to complete the test which could be a lot more time to spend for most people. This is the only weakness of the test. Besides that, the test can be easily purchased at $10 which is a fair amount for the test. https://www.enneagramworldwide.com/test/

6. Eclectic Energies Enneagram Tests

Eclectic Energies Enneagram Tests is present in two variations. It can be a classical enneagram test or the enneagram test with the instinctual variation. Both tests are free of cost and can be used to get the best results for the personality types. They provide deep and insightful questions to determine the right personality type.

https://www.eclecticenergies.com/enneagram/test

7. Composite Enneagram Test

Composite Enneagram Test is another option that the people could avail if they are looking to get any free Enneagram test with fairly good results. There are a deep sequence of insightful questions with 5 options each asked in the test for each personality characteristics to determine the right type of the personality.

http://davesenneagram.com/test/composite-enneagram-test

The results are a great evaluation of your true self and will help to determine personality of you and your partner. Based on the results, you can bring positive changes in your life. It is recommended by the psychologists to take this as an over the counter psychological evaluation and no medication or therapy should be conducted based on the results. It is a preliminary evaluation and will develop a baseline for further psychological evaluations.

How to evaluate your partner's and family members' personality?

Enneagram test is a great way to check personality compatibility with your partner and your family members. If you want to know the personality type of your partner or your family members, you can easily avail any of the above mentioned personality test and ask them to fill in the questionnaires. The personality type results will be a great aid in depicting if you are compatible with your partner or not.

There are compatibility tests based in relationships in the Enneagram test types. The main aim of these test is to provide an insight into the type of personalities you should date. If you are single and looking to date someone, take the Enneagram which are as follows.

1. The Enneagram compatibility Test by Millennial Grind

The Compatibility Enneagram test by millennial grind is one of the most popular ones among the millennial. The main reason of the popularity is the fact that people find it difficult to date someone who is compatible with them. The test is only 10 minutes long and has 15 questions which are based on the relationship choices that you make and what personality type you should date. If you are already dating someone, you should do this test to check your compatibility.

https://millennial-grind.com/free-enneagram-compatibility-test-what-type-should-you-date/

2. The compatibility of Enneagram types in Love by Mind Journal

Mind Journal also provides the compatibility test fir the Enneagram types where you can easily find the compatibility of your personality type with the other types. The strengths and weaknesses of each personality type with each of the other personality types are provided so that you can easily see if you are with the right person or not. It should be just taken in the fun perspective and no life based decisions should be made based on that.

https://themindsjournal.com/the-compatibility-of-enneagram-types-in-love/?amp

Chapter 3: Enneagram tests and its types

Enneagram test is based on the figures where nine types are given to the personality. These types provide of an overview of the personality that a person might have depending on the answers given in the test. Each personality type imposes different sets of qualities in a person which may vary with the passage of time. A detailed overview of what each personality type brings will be provided in the sections below for an effective analysis.

What your enneagram type says about you (type 1-3)

TYPE 1: THE REFORMER AND PERFECTIONIST

Perfectionist and reformers are the people who are the number one type of personality and are based on integrity and self-control. Their aim is to do the right thing, amend the wrongdoings and bring integrity, honesty, wisdom and trust to work. They are the responsible individuals who want other people to take responsibility in life like they do. They set high values and standards for themselves in life and are very binary in their approach. Since they tend to simplify things, they work hard and prefer quality over quantity of work. They are very critical of others and themselves, idealistic in nature and work hard to improve the world around them. They act as social reformers. They can achieve self-betterment by accepting their imperfections and learning to grow despite resistances.

Strengths: Trustable, Honest, responsible, growth-driven

Issues: Offended and annoyed easily, rigid, and very critical

Habits and emotions: They are very accurate and detail-oriented in their speaking and approach. While they are hardworking, they have a tendency of being resentful and rigid in their approach. They need to develop a sense of serenity to ensure that they are able to accept the imperfections in their lives effectively, are able to let go and deal with anger in a proper manner since they are a body-based type. They have to put their health first. Since they are very grounded and practical in their approach, they aim to develop a perfect self-image. By being more accepting, they can excel in life.

TYPE 2: THE HELPER

The helper is the second types of personality based on the Enneagram test. It is a feeling-based type and its most highlight and focus is on the relationships which a person is able to make. Such a person is able to make successful relationships and connections with people. His socializing skills allow him to excel in developing the skills of empathy and fulfilling and understanding the needs and feelings of the people related to him in his professional and personal life. The type two people are expert at supporting others and aiding in creating a sense of motivation and praise to help people to raise above their potential. Such people are not self-centered. It is hard for them to focus on themselves and understand the needs of their own. In order to earn the liking and approval of others, they work had to adapt to the changing circumstances and improve themselves effectively.

However, they tend to have a sensitive soul which makes them adsorb whatever others offer to them. It is difficult for them to be angry or develop effective personal limits. They may experience emotional outbursts to get rid of the pressure.

Strengths: Helpful, caring, communicating experts, expert interpersonal skills

Issues: Lack of self-care, fortunate, naive, highly dependent

Emotions and habits: They are very helpful and nice and come off as sympathetic. This allows them to give advice and counseling people which is a great way to motivate them to excel in their lives. They have a feeling of being proud since they think that they are better than others. They might develop a sense of poor self-esteem if they are not given the right appraisal all the times. They experience humility since they sometimes question their self-worth due to excessive self-judgment. Such people disregard their own feelings while trying to help others and repress their feelings in doing so. There is a buildup of energy, as well as tension in such individuals which make them less grounded. They tend to get anxious easily and this emotion might effectively cover all the other emotions. They must ensure that their energy keeps them grounded.

TYPE 3: THE PERFORMER

The third type of personality is the performer. This is the feeling-based type. This type of people make sure that they use their emotional energy to get acts and things done effectively. They are always keen to take the initiative. They are hard workers and make sure that they complete their goals and aims. Since they try to get things done, they have a lot of flexibility and adaptability in their nature. They excel at meeting the expectations of the superiors. They are very active and optimistic in their approach. They are very hard to stop and slow down once they set out to achieve some aim. They are hard to keep away from their goals and they tend to overlook their health and everything concerned when it comes to their goals.

Since they are very productive and effective in their approach towards life and their work, they bring a lot of positive reinforcement for people who work for them and with them. The main issue that they face is the need for external praise which makes them loose self-esteem and confidence. They don't adapt easily or step out of their roles.

Strengths: Active, successful, energetic, high achiever

Issues: Low self-esteem, over worked, impulsive, competitive

Emotions and habits: Since they are very energetic, enthusiastic, and motivating for others and themselves, there is a sense of approval and vanity which they seek from others. They have a sense of truthfulness which makes them to develop a lot of personal authenticity. They tend to worry about their image in the eyes of others. In order to ensure that they succeed, they don't accept defeat easily and try to maintain a picture of self-image of being "successful." There is a sense of tension and anxiety due to the stress and pressure. They tend to be sad despite the professional outcomes which are always good.

What your enneagram type says about you (type 4-6)

TYPE 4: THE INDIVIDUALIST

The individualists are the personality type number 4. They belong to the feeling-based types. Such people have a sense of longing and desire. There is a sense of deprivation in them and a quest for something. They develop a deep sense of envy as well as idealism about their lives. They are very detail oriented. They are creative and seek the same sort of passion from other people as well.

The type four are very artistic and free spirited. They seek a career in dance, music, and poetry. They want to have a good image while being real. They tend to be alone and seek happiness and satisfaction more from their self rather than people.

Strengths: Very Compassionate, committed, emotionally stable

Issues: Very Moody, detached, rigid in nature

Emotions and habits: They can be warm and loving as well as happy but they cannot seek a balance in that. They become detached and lonely very easily. There is a sense of disappointment in them. They need to develop calmness to be open to feelings while projecting the right image for themselves and being passionate and happy as well in their emotional state.

TYPE 5: THE INVESTIGATOR

This is the fifth type of personality which belongs to the mental types. They are the people always focus on the acquiring of knowledge because to them the most important thing is being intellectual and being knowledgeable. They can make a great career as scholars and analysts. They pay attention to details and have a special talent to link things together and draw conclusions. They seek privacy in their lives and personal freedom is integral to them as well. They are intellectually superb and are heavy knowledgeable as well. But they are very detached so making relationships is a big challenge for them. For them, work is the main priority and family or friends come later.

Strengths: Knowledgeable, insightful, and self-sufficient

Issues: Detached, critical, stressful

Emotions and habit: Fives are very critical and technical in their approach towards everything. They are very big talkers of their favorite topics. They tend to be very stressful of what they know. For them, it is not easy to share anything at all. They consider it as a loss of knowledge to themselves. There is a sense of detachment from the rest of the world in their nature. They must consider their feelings and participate in the little things in life. Isolation is the emotion that they need to cut down in life. They tend to develop an overly possessive attitude about their image which can create a sense of emptiness. They must bring their attention to other people and their emotions. They must create a sense of sensitivity in their lives.

TYPE 6: THE LOYALIST

What your enneagram type says about you (type 7-9)

TYPE 7: THE ENTHUSIAST

The enthusiast are the seventh personality type. It belongs to the mental type and is a group of people who are forward thinkers. They are the ones who are active in life and like to get things done. They are very optimistic and have a very positive attitude about life. They tend to seek knowledge about everything and do not set any limits for themselves. They have great interpersonal skills. They don't care about what people think of them. They have an adventurous spirit and they love to travel. They love new technologies and love new ideas, intellectual pursuits as well as pleasurable feelings.

Strengths: Free spirited, adventurous, enthusiastic, forward thinkers

Issues: Self-absorbed, distracted, casual

Emotions and habits: They are the people who have a personality like telling a story and are very self-absorbed as well. They are optimistic as well. They are fun loving and easy going in their lives. However, they can be clingy at times which means that they can be too occupied with their ideas at times which might not be compatible with other people. They must seek sobriety in their lives.

TYPE 8: THE CHALLENGER

The challengers or the Eights are composed of a body-based personality type. They are born leaders. They take challenges heads on. They are very energetic and dominating in their approach. They might come off as intimidating as well but they seek achieving the results and leading to get results. With control, they seek to be better. They are effective decision makers. They seek justice and if it is not given, they fight back for it. They are bold and aggressive but their boldness makes them admirable.

Strengths: Passionate, generous, and bold

Problems: Controlling, aggressive, dominating

Emotions and habits: The challengers are very bold and assertive in their approach towards everything in life. They are very controlling and bossy as well. But they are effective decision makers which is a great trait to have. They can be aggressive but they achieve things with their leadership. They must have to explore the innocent side of their lives as well as open-mindedness. They might seek an effort to make an image for themselves which is a sign of stress since they want approval from people which is not a healthy approach to life. They are very energetic in life and assert control over things to make them work the right way. They might be over-worked. They need to control their anger and aggression in life.

TYPE 9: THE PEACEMAKER

The peacemakers are the ninth personality type and is the most common one as well. They hold the people together. They have a tendency to be flexible in life. They keep people together while making sure that work is done effectively. They tend to look after the needs of others while ignoring themselves. They are the mediators and create an environment of trust and feasibility.

Strengths: Generous, compliant, and affable

Issues: Rigid, hesitant, conflict avoidant

Habits and emotions: These are the people who are very welcoming but they land themselves in trouble due to this. They are too persuasive and distracted as well. They don't put attention to detail and are rigid in their approach as well. They don't have any personal priorities and they avoid conflicts to make sure that they have a good image. They might not be as optimistic and as active as the other signs and they try to blend in. There is a sense of laziness in them. There is a need for them to develop effective boundaries for a better approach to life.

Chapter 4: Criticism faced by the test

There has been a significant amount of criticism which the Enneagram test has to face. As mentioned above a lot of times that it is not an authentic test and it should not be considered a final word in any case, there are issues and criticism which is based on the facts that the test has been growing. The major ones are listed below:

Lack of a sound psychological background

The test is not based on any psychological theory. While many theories and tests like Myers Briggs Personality Tests, Big Five Personality test and DISC has some psychological background and yet they face severe backlash due to the results and the lack of validity, the Enneagram test has no validity from the psychologist. There is no theory that supports the test which is a big issue and criticism which it faces.

Clash with nature

It has been established by psychologists who have laid the focus on the behavioral and cognitive theories for the development of the personalities and behaviors. Since these theories focus on the evolution of the personality based on the age, environment, surroundings and the gender of the person as well, the enneagram test is well in contraindication with the psychological theories. It tries to identify and explain personalities based on the answers given while the theories are based on research and studies. This has received a lot of criticism from the professionals since people have been considering this test as a sound and professional recommendation which is a sign.

No sound history

It has been wrongly established that Gurdjieff gave this theory of essence which is used in the test. However, the test is not able to establish the sound theoretical basis which is needed to establish that the test is actually based on the theory. The test does not give any personality development based on the essence theory suggested but Gurdjieff. It is not connected to the psychological theories as well in any manner so without having a sound history and background, it is hard to establish that the test is valid.

Making significant decisions based on the test

The test suggest to bring changes in the life of a person based on the personality. This is the approach which has been criticized the most by the experts. Since people may make life decisions based on the test, it is a lack of narrative which brings the criticism to the test. Since no psychological theory is able to explain the narrative of the test, it must not be considered a valid factor to make the significant life decisions.

Need to fit in

The test makes people to fit in the nine types which the test is composed of. There are significant challenges in this and the criticism arises from the fact that there are different aspects of personality which one person has from another so fitting them all together in the nine types is a thing to consider. Many psychologist view this as a major limitation.

Lack of research

There is a pick and choose approach to the test which makes people to choose the answers according to the personality type that they want to have. Since there are tons of free questionnaires available on the internet, it is easy to modify the test according to the likings of a person. The lack of research on the centers, wings or subtypes as well as the lack of explanation about the development of personality is a major reason that the authenticity and validity of the test are challenged.

Chapter 5: Enneagram tests and its role in detecting suitable career options

Many people consider this test as a basis to determine the career type in which they will be successful. You don't want to be an introvert and want to be a salesperson since it is clearly a contraindicated job for your personality. The above nine types give a whole new perspective if they are taken into consideration for choosing the right career for a person. The suggestions are however based on the traits of the person. The suggestions are general and must not be considered as an absolute answer to all the psychological queries or career selection methods.

Type 1 (The Perfectionist)

A perfectionist is someone who is very methodological and detail oriented. They are very competitive and focused as well. Being independent in their work, they tend to be great leader and managers. They can have a great role in medicine, law, QA and QC in any field as well as IT managers. Their ability to manage and do things to perfections is an aid for them in their career whatever they choose to do.

Type 2 (The Helper)

Being a generous and people's person, a helper will be a person who will be in a profession where they can help others. The healthcare and medical profession is a great career for such people. They can be great psychologists and therapists as well as counselors.

Type 3 (The Achiever)

An achiever is someone who is always after the success. They will be very sophisticated and accomplished with a skillset to impress anyone. They have a high-profile position and tend to stand out among the crowd since they are ambitious and eager to achieve things in life. They have a great career and future in the entertainment, business, communications, sports and coaching industry.

Type 4 (The Individualist)

An individualist will be at his best when there are risks and restrictions since they are creative and try to find solutions in less resources. They can be great designers, architects, writers, artists in dancing and singing, as well as painters.

Type 5 (The Investigator)

An investigator is a person who is able to make connections between different aspects, they note short details. They tend to be much focused and are often detached from the world as well. A job as an analyst, economists, investigator, scientist, researcher and writer are the ones which will suite such people.

Type 6 (The Loyalist)

The loyalist is a person who is very precise, Practical, and creative. They pay special attention to details and have the ability to deal with the crisis. Being the troubleshooters, they try to solve every problem. They can be creators and careers as computer programming, finance management, law, research, and security are recommended for them.

Type 7 (The Enthusiast)

Such people are full of creativity and enthusiasm. They bring a lot of innovation and open-minded ness to the group where they work. They love to work with people and have the ability to be social while managing their careers. They must choose a career in profession like Public relations, sales and marketing, archaeology, and travel writing. They have an artistic side to discover as well in their profession.

Type 8 (The Challenger)

Challenger is someone who the one is making decisions. He has to be the leader of whatever he does. He is bold, daring and a leader who can take decisions heads on. A career as an entrepreneur in any field is full of risks and a challenger has the potential to fulfill those risks. As well as the careers in business management, politics, or national intelligence agencies is a great option as well.

Type 9 (The Peacemaker)

Peace is a common feature of the social service workers, nurses and volunteers in many fields. Alongside that, the fields of arts and humanitarian sciences are filed with people who are ideal for making peace. There are fairly high chances for a peacemaker to make career as writers, artists, nurses, social workers as well as a partially successful career in counselling, human resources, architecture, and teaching in the humanities as well.

Conclusion

Enneagram test is a great and a fun-loving personality test that could prove beneficial for you in your life. As much interesting as it sounds, it should not be taken as a measure for testing personality and making life decision upon it. Since there is a lack of research and evidence on the basis of which the results are provided in the test and lack of correlation of the test with the personality theories and literature, the test in no ways is an alternate for a proper psychological evaluation if any medical condition persists. Enneagram test is a great way to engage with your family, made positive additions to your personality and amend your relationships in a positive manner without taking anything negative or attaining any negative aspects from the tests.

-- [April Alexander]